Austin

a photographic journey

photography by John R Rogers and Rob Greebon
text by Mike Cox

FARCOUNTRY PRESS

On May 25th, 2015, a devastating storm passed through Austin and central Texas causing the loss of many lives and hundreds of homes. As the storm moved out of the area, the sun broke through the turbulent sky to create a truly spectacular sunset allowing me to photograph the cover image "After the Storm."

I'd like to dedicate "Austin: A Photographic Journey" to all first responders that brave the storms and allow the rest of us to feel safe and enjoy the beauty around us.
—John R Rogers

To Rachel and Katie—the lights of my life.
—Rob Greebon

Right: If any image is symbolic of Austin, it is this: the 1880s-vintage capitol in the background with the rotunda of the statehouse's modern underground extension in the foreground. The capital of Texas is grounded in the past, but with its universities, high-tech industries, and ever-changing skyline, Austin continues to move into the future. Rob Greebon

Title page: Downtown Austin stands on the north side of the Colorado River, now dammed to create the city's figurative crown jewel, Lady Bird Lake. Rob Greebon

Front cover: Austin, the nation's eleventh-largest city and Texas' fourth largest, is a place where icon meets idea. It's a city of cutting-edge innovation and well-known landmarks. John R Rogers

Back cover: When the Republic of Texas decided to build the young nation's capital at the frontier village of Waterloo on the Colorado River, the stream could only be crossed by riding a horse or in a wagon across the shallows. Today, six bridges bind the north and south sides of the city, including the graceful through-arch Pennybacker Bridge, also known as the Loop 360 Bridge. Rob Greebon

ISBN: 978-1-56037-663-7

© 2016 by Farcountry Press
Photography © 2016 by John R Rogers
Photography © 2016 by Rob Greebon
Text by Mike Cox

For more information about our books, write Farcountry Press, P.O. Box 5630, Helena, MT 59604; call (800) 821-3874; or visit www.farcountrypress.com.

Produced in the United States of America.
Printed in China.

20 19 18 17 16   1 2 3 4 5 6

Right: The GuitarTown Project began in 2006 with the placing of numerous colorfully painted Gibson guitars around the city. Most of those pieces of public art were auctioned the following year to raise money to benefit nonprofit organizations in Austin, but three remain on Congress Avenue and seven at Bergstrom International Airport. Shown here is the work called *Vibrancy*, located at 4th Street and Congress. John R Rogers

Far right: Opened in 1915 as the Majestic Theater and later renamed the Paramount, Austin's original performing arts venue has stood the test of time, offering entertainment to the community for over 100 years. The classical Revival-style structure was listed on the National Register of Historic Places in 1976. John R Rogers

Below: Originally known as Pecan Street, Sixth Street is Austin's Bourbon Street. Visitors and locals alike flock to the street for world-class food, fun watering holes, and entertainment ranging from comedy to live music of every genre. John R Rogers

Above: The late blues guitarist Stevie Ray Vaughan cast a long shadow on Austin's world-renowned live music scene, and so does this bronze statue of him on the south side of Lady Bird Lake just off Riverside Drive. Cast from a sculpture by Ralph Helmick, the statue went up in 1993. Rob Greebon

Right: The Art Deco-style six open-spandrel concrete arch Lamar Boulevard Bridge on Lady Bird Lake is a historic bridge that was added to the National Register of Historic Places in 1994. The graceful landmark bridge appears to float on the misty water on this pastel sunrise morning. Rob Greebon

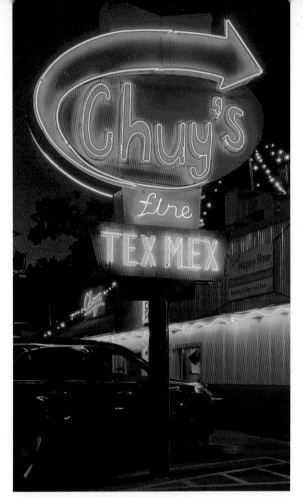

Left: Tex-Mex is one of Austin's three basic food groups, the others being barbecue and chicken-fried steak. Chuy's is one of many eateries in the capital offering that special blend of hot and spicy cuisine that came to be known as Tex-Mex. Rob Greebon

Far left: The Broken Spoke opened in 1964 as a country western dance hall and eatery on the southern edge of the city. The list of noted entertainers who have played here ranges from Bob Wills and His Texas Playboys to Willie Nelson. Austin has long since spread way beyond the Spoke, as locals call it, but the music goes on as the Lone Star beer and chicken-fried steak goes down. John R Rogers

Below: Franklin Barbecue has become an Austin tradition. Their business model is simple: "Starting at 11 a.m., we will sell 'cue until we run out—and then we close for the day." It's so good, people are willing to stand in line for hours to eat here and often find it's sold out by the time their turn comes up. Even presidents of the United States have been known to drop by for some 'cue when they're in town. John R Rogers

Above: Austin has scores of public art pieces, from statues to murals to fanciful works that are hard to classify other than to say they are eye-catching. This fiberglass longhorn, twelve feet tall and with a nine-foot horn spread, permanently grazes behind the University of Texas Co-Op just across from the UT campus. Rob Greebon

Right: The University of Texas at Austin's West Mall area is often used as a rally space for students. At night, the top of the iconic UT Tower is often bathed in orange light in salute of important occasions, from athletic and academic victories to graduation day. Whenever UT wins a national championship in any collegiate sport, the whole tower is lit orange, with office lights making a giant "1." Rob Greebon

Above: Spotlights keep the historic state capitol illuminated all night. The city of Austin was founded in 1839 as capital of the Republic of Texas and remained the seat of government after Texas became the twenty-eighth state of the union in 1845. Rob Greebon

Right: Like the song says, "The stars at night are big and bright / Deep in the heart of Texas." This is a composite showing what the Milky Way would look like above the Loop 360 bridge over Lake Austin if the lights of the city were not so bright. Rob Greebon

Above: Oblivious to joggers and walkers passing nearby on the hike-and-bike trail, a solitary swan enjoys a leisurely swim beneath the Lamar Boulevard Bridge spanning Lady Bird Lake. Rob Greebon

Left: The boardwalk portion of the Ann and Roy Butler Hike-and-Bike Trail around Lady Bird Lake opened in 2014. With completion of this link, it became possible to take a ten-mile run, walk, or bike ride around the lake. Annually, more than 1.5 million people take advantage of the trail, one of Austin's most popular recreation features.
John R Rogers

GABLES.
5TH STREET
COMMONS

KEEP BLADE S

ESTERN

MEAN-EYED CAT BAR

HE DRESSED LIKE A HIP CORONER & SANG LIKE A GUNMAN TURNED PENTECOSTAL PREACHER

BEER & WINE
TO-GO
SUNDAY-FRIDAY til MIDNITE
SATURDAYS til 1am

OPEN
MON-THURS
5PM-2am
WEEKENDS
2PM-2am

SAT
MARK STUART
+ THE BASTARD SONS
(9-10)
WEST COAST HANDS
(8-10)

NO MINORS

WE SHARPEN
CHAIN SAWS

1 6 2 1

MAILBOX

THE MERCY SEAT

MEAN AS HELL

YOU BEAT ALL I EVER SAW

Above: Art in Austin is found in museums, galleries, and many non-traditional venues. This eccentric mixed-media piece of privately owned public art is located behind a retail establishment on South Lamar Boulevard. John R Rogers

Left: This eight-foot-tall statue of singer-songwriter Willie Nelson began its everlasting gig in 2011 in front of the then-new Austin City Limits Live studio at the Moody Theater. Philadelphia artist Clete Shields spent three years on the project, producing a dozen versions in clay before settling on this design.
John R Rogers

Far left: The eclectic Mean-Eyed Cat Bar got its name from the 1950s Johnny Cash song about a blue-eyed blonde and her mean-eyed cat. Opened in 2004, the bar features local brews and 'cue. Rob Greebon

Next pages: Looking southwest at sunset from above the Percy V. Pennybacker Jr. Bridge, the striking weathered-steel through-arch structure carries vehicles using the Loop 360 Highway, also called the Capital of Texas Highway. Rob Greebon

Above: Visitors deplaning at Austin's Bergstrom International Airport often are greeted by the sound of music (jazz, rock, or country, not the movie score!) from a live performance. If no music is scheduled at a particular time, this public art array in the baggage claim area illustrates that Austin considers itself the "Live Music Capital of the World." John R Rogers

Left: From the Long Center for the Performing Arts on the south side of Lady Bird Lake, visitors enjoy a stunning view of Austin's skyline. John R Rogers

Right: The Santa Rita No. 1 is a historic drilling rig on the University of Texas campus. On May 28, 1923, this discovery well struck oil, revealing the riches below the surface of the remote desolate lands set aside by the Texas Legislature for the university. The oil profits helped make UT one of the best-funded universities in the nation. The rig was moved to its current location in 1958. John R Rogers

Far right: Austin is a vibrant and fast-growing city, but it hasn't lost touch with its colorful past. The Bob Bullock Texas State History Museum tells the story of Texas, a saga in which Austin's history is thoroughly entwined. Rob Greebon

Below: This massive monument on the state capitol grounds, dedicated in 2012, honors Texas' rich Hispanic heritage. In the early 1730s, Spain operated three missions near present-day Barton Springs. John R Rogers

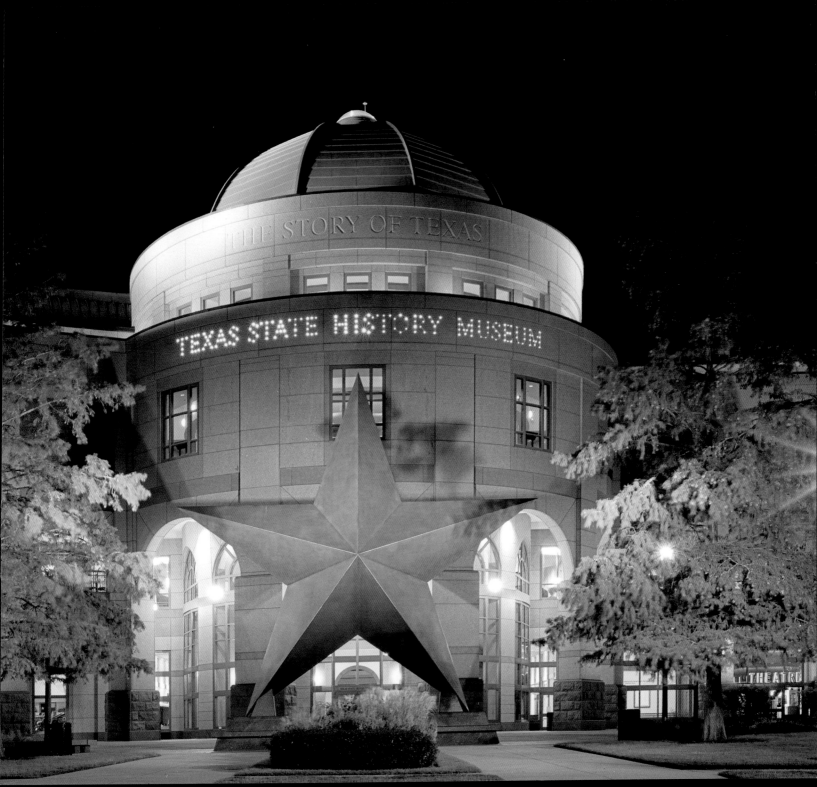

Left: Vast fields of sweet-smelling spring bluebonnets can turn the Austin-area landscape blue. The more rain in the fall and winter, the more prolific the bluebonnets. Rob Greebon

Below: Although the Texas Legislature did not name the bluebonnet as the official state flower until 1901, bluebonnets and paintbrushes are as old as the proverbial hills. John R Rogers

Above: For 130 years, the historic Driskill Hotel has hosted Texas' and many of the nation's most noted and influential people, from stage and film stars to presidents. When you walk into the bar, you'll know you are in Texas with the star-studded stained-glass dome and carpet, comfortable leather sofas, and the bronze *Widow Maker* sculpture by Barvo Walker. John R Rogers

Right: Austin visitors have been staying and dining at the Driskill Hotel since it opened in 1886. Graced with Romanesque arches and balconies, and built of light-colored brick and locally quarried limestone, the four-story hotel in the heart of downtown has seen much of the city's history and continues to accommodate visitors to the capital. John R Rogers

Above: You don't have to go inside a restaurant to enjoy Austin-style cuisine. With food truck vendors offering everything from gyros to sausage wraps to cupcakes, the capital is a foodie's paradise. John R Rogers

Left: If there's anything better than the food at the popular Oasis Restaurant on Lake Travis, it's the spectacular sunsets viewed from the restaurant's terraces. Perched on a cliff 450 feet above the lake, the Oasis is one of the largest restaurants in the world, and is an excellent location to watch the activity on the lake.

Lake Travis is a popular recreational reservoir on the Colorado River created by the Mansfield Dam. It is the largest of the area's reservoirs at over 63 miles long and with 270 miles of shoreline, and is popular for swimming, boating, fishing, and camping. The lake also generates electricity, serves as a water supply for Austin, and is the primary flood control reservoir of the Highland Lakes chain. John R Rogers

Right: Former first lady Claudia Taylor (Lady Bird) Johnson and actress Helen Hayes founded the National Wildflower Research Center in 1982. Now known as the Lady Bird Johnson Wildflower Center, its gardens showcase native Texas wildflowers and other fauna. The center is dedicated to helping preserve the state's varied plant life, and in 2006, became a research unit of the University of Texas. John R Rogers

Far right: Metropolitan Austin covers most of Travis County, but there's still enough farm and ranch land to accommodate livestock, such as this mare and her colt in a field of wildflowers. Rob Greebon

Next pages: Austin's ever-changing skyline has inspired the long-standing joke that Austin's official bird should be the "construction crane." Rob Greebon

Below: Texas bluebonnets and other wildflowers decorate the Loop 360 Highway on its way to the Pennybacker Bridge. Rob Greebon

Above: Austin has many miles of hike-and-bike trails used year-round, including the ten-mile Ann and Roy Butler Hike-and-Bike Trail around Lady Bird Lake. John R Rogers

Right: One of Austin-area's most scenic places, Hamilton Pool is fed by a 50-foot waterfall on Hamilton Creek, about three-quarters of a mile upstream from the Pedernales River. Home to a population of threatened golden-cheeked warblers, the popular swimming hole and surrounding acreage became a nature preserve in 1990. John R Rogers

Below: Located in the basin area of Lake Travis, McGregor Park, more commonly known as Hippie Hollow Park, has a rugged shoreline made up of steep rocky limestone steps which offer beautiful views of the lake. Its remote location made it a popular place in the 1960s and 1970s for skinny dipping and nude sunbathing, and now Hippie Hollow is the only clothing-optional public park in Texas. John R Rogers

Above: The Joe R. and Teresa Lozano Long Center for the Performing Arts is home to many of Austin's local arts organizations. Over 80 percent of their performances feature local artists. Rob Greebon

Left: The Texas State Capitol stands at the head of Congress Avenue. Clearly, a lot has changed since 1838, when Republic of Texas President Mirabeau Lamar hunted buffalo here. Rob Greebon

Next pages: Down on South Lamar is Maria's Taco Xpress, a South Austin icon known for its homemade tacos and funky *Hippie Opera* mural by local folk artist Michael Peschka. Several times a week, the establishment features live music, but on Sundays, Maria's serves Sunday Gospel Brunch and is called "Hippie Church" by locals. Rob Greebon

CORBALANS
EMPORIUM
HIPPIE OPERA
ESTABLIS
1996
OPERA
HOUSE
JAIL
GENERAL
STORE
TICKETS
FIRE LANE, TOW AWAY ZONE

Above: The city maintains Mount Bonnell as one of its many municipal parks. Technically, it's called Covert Park and features this pavilion at the top, stone steps, and other amenities dating back to 1939. With its romantic lover's leap legend and spectacular views, the landmark has been attracting people since before recorded history. John R Rogers

Left: Mount Bonnell offers expansive sunset views of Lake Austin and beyond. A peak only a Texan could call a mountain, the prominence used to be Austin's highest point at 780 feet above sea level. But as the city grew to the northwest, it encompassed land with an elevation of more than 1,100 feet. Rob Greebon

Right: All Saints Episcopal Church opened in 1882 on what was then the far north edge of Austin. Seventeen years later, this limestone house of worship was completed. Listed on the National Register of Historic Places, it is one of Austin's oldest churches, located near the University of Texas campus. John R Rogers

Far right: The Texas Governor's Mansion, built five years before the Civil War in 1856, stands at 11th and Colorado Streets, just to the southwest of the capitol. Among the mansion's many noted occupants were former Republic of Texas President Sam Houston and U.S. President George W. Bush. John R Rogers

Below: The oldest wood-framed structure in Austin, the French Legation Museum in East Austin, went up in 1841 as a private residence for French chargé d'affaires Alphonse Dubois during Texas' time as an independent republic. Today the property is owned by the state and operated as a museum by the Daughters of the Republic of Texas. John R Rogers

Above: The city's Trail of Lights in Zilker Park annually brightens Austin's holiday celebrations, literally and figuratively. John R Rogers

Right: A large Christmas tree (grown in Texas, of course) shines bright in front of the state capitol on a cool, rainy December morning before sunrise. Rob Greebon

Below: Before automobiles replaced horses, Austinites traveled around town in carriages and other wagons. Now the carriage-ride option is back, with tours or romantic nighttime soirees available. Rob Greebon

Right: Looking up from the rotunda to the interior dome of the state capitol, one will see the state's iconic lone star with the word "Texas" surrounding it. Although it looks small when standing under the dome, the star actually measures eight feet in diameter. Rob Greebon

Far right: The senate chamber is on the second floor of the capitol's east wing. Restored in an extensive renovation from 1990 to 1995, the chamber was returned to its original 1905 appearance with the 31 original walnut desks created for the senate in 1888, and replicas of the original finishes. Rob Greebon

Below: Austin's capitol is known for its architectural beauty inside and out, and the great attention to detail is also seen in the staircases which are embellished with intricately carved wood and painted details. Rob Greebon

Previous pages: Austin's downtown skyline with bridges over a calm Lady Bird Lake looks at rest on this moonlit evening. However, as one of the fastest growing cities in America, this skyline is always on the move—up, that is, with new skyscrapers to accommodate the city's dynamic business and residential growth. More than 912,000 people call Austin home—many of them living in high-rise condos in the central area of the city. John R Rogers

Left: Stephen F. Austin, the man considered the father of Anglo Texas and the namesake of the capital, died in 1836 and was buried in Brazoria County. His remains were moved to the Texas State Cemetery in 1910. John R Rogers

Below: In 1842, Republic of Texas President Sam Houston ordered the removal of all government records from Austin. That would have amounted to abandoning the then-village as the republic's capital, and the citizenry did not like that idea. Locals resisted with arms, and while no one got hurt, the archives stayed in Austin. This statue near Sixth Street and Congress Avenue honors Angelina Eberly, who legend has it touched off a cannon to alert Austin's citizens, who then prevented Texas Rangers from completing their assignment. John R Rogers

Above: Few places in Texas offer a prettier body of water for kayaking and canoeing than Austin. But don't bring your power boat—gasoline motors are not allowed on Lady Bird Lake. Rob Greebon

Right: The Gulf of Mexico is some 150 miles from Austin, but that doesn't mean the city doesn't have sandy places to have fun in the sun.
John R Rogers

Facing page: On a hot summer day, Barton Springs Pool in Zilker Park offers relief from the heat with 69-degree spring-fed water. Diehard swimmers even use the pool in the winter. John R Rogers

Next pages: Opened in 1924 as Texas Memorial Stadium, the University of Texas at Austin's Darrell K. Royal Stadium is home to the Longhorns, named after the majestic cattle felt to embody the strength of Texas. Rob Greebon

Above: One of Austin's several slogans is "Keep Austin Weird." Originally developed to support local businesses, the slogan has also been proudly embraced by the community as symbolic of their diversity and eccentricity. The "Kung Fu Grip" graffiti painting on the Austin Railroad Bridge over Lady Bird Lake is just one example of Austin's self-proclaimed weirdness. Rob Greebon

Right: Another of Austin's alternative public art venues that embraces the city's "spirit of weird" is Graffiti Park on Baylor at Castle Hill. Not really a park, it's where local artists turned the walls of an abandoned building site into colorful, ever-changing canvases. Rob Greebon

Far right: Sixth Street is home to the city's annual South by Southwest Festival (SXSW), as well as other annual events, from Pecan Street Art Festival to Halloween night to Mardi Gras, for which the thoroughfare is temporarily closed for the crowds that flood the street.
John R Rogers

57

Above: One of nineteen monuments on the state capitol grounds, this statue by renowned sculptor Pompeo Coppini of horse and rider honors "Terry's Texas Rangers," the Eighth Texas Calvary unit who served during the Civil War in the Provisional Army of the Confederate States.
John R Rogers

Right: Not only do tens of thousands of people work in Austin's bustling downtown during the day, but multiple thousands have also chosen to forsake lawn mowing in suburbia to live an urban lifestyle amongst the bustling activity and cultural riches of the city. John R Rogers

Above: High school football is a big deal in Austin on Friday nights. In fact, much of the popular TV series *Friday Night Lights* was shot here during the show's 2006-2011 run. The film crews are gone, but schoolboy football continues to provide future talent for college and university teams across the state. John R Rogers

Left: You can do just about anything in Texas' fast-growing, fourth-largest city, including taking a ride in a hot-air balloon. John R Rogers

Far left: The Circuit of The Americas racetrack, opened in 2012 near the small community of Elroy just outside Austin, hosts the Formula 1 Grand Prix and other major motorcar and motorcycle events each year. The Grand Prix brings fast-car enthusiasts to Austin from around the world. John R Rogers

Above: Perched high on the cliffs of Lake Travis, the view is spectacular from St. Luke's on the Lake Episcopal Church. John R Rogers

Right: The 36th president of the United States, Texan Lyndon B. Johnson, chose Austin as the location for housing his papers and memorabilia. Opened in 1971, the LBJ Presidential Library and Museum draws visitors from all over the nation and the world. Among the many exhibits is a replica of the Oval Office as it appeared during Johnson's years in the White House. John R Rogers

Far right: Originally named Town Lake, this reservoir on the Colorado River was renamed in honor of Claudia Taylor (Lady Bird) Johnson. Following her husband's presidency, Mrs. Johnson played a key role in the beautification of Lady Bird Lake. Rob Greebon

Above: The interior of Austin's modernistic City Hall takes advantage of natural daylight with its shiny copper ceiling that reflects light from the building's many windows to its large gathering space. The windows also offer beautiful views of Lady Bird Lake. John R Rogers

Left: Built of native Texas limestone and mostly recycled copper, the seat of local government was built very "green," with an exterior of angled, multi-level terraces inspired by the natural landscape of the hill country and the cool, informal vibe of the city. To incorporate history, a sapling from Austin's famous 500-year-old "Treaty Oak" was planted in the plaza. Rob Greebon

Above: Everything's big in Texas—except the "Tiniest Bar in Texas." Though the bar is as small as its name suggests, it features live entertainment on the patio behind it and a food trailer for "eats." Rob Greebon

Right: Austinites don't need much of an excuse to organize a festival of some kind. Sixth Street is the heart of the entertainment district, offering live music nightly and festivals throughout the year. John R Rogers

Below: The painted bull at the Long Center of the Performing Arts is one of Austin's many pieces of colorful public art. In 1985, the city became one of the first in the nation to establish a public arts office as a function of municipal government. John R Rogers

Previous pages: The daily bat flight from beneath the Congress Avenue Bridge has long-since eclipsed the once better known event at Carlsbad Caverns National Park. The bridge hosts the largest urban bat colony in North America. Bat-watching season is from early March to early November. Rob Greebon

Right: Austin is a city on the move, literally. Every April, thousands of people take part in the Statesman Capitol 10,000, also known as Cap10K, which has become the largest 10K run in Texas and one of the largest in the nation. Most run in the race, but many walk it, sometimes in costumes or personalized t-shirts, just to be a part of this fun Austin spring ritual. John R Rogers

Below: Austin's not San Francisco, but sometimes it does get foggy. Here, the Pennybacker Bridge on Loop 360 disappears into the fog rising from Lake Austin. Rob Greebon

70

Above: One of the hipper parts of town is along South Congress Avenue. This revitalized area known as SoCo features eclectic shops and antique stores, hip eateries and food trucks, and cool entertainment and art venues just south of downtown Austin. Rob Greebon

Left: The capital has a substantial year-round population of pink flamingos, the largest flock gracing the roadside in the vicinity of Loop 360 and Bee Cave Road—although in Austin, the flock is all-plastic. Rob Greebon

Far left: The confluence of spring-fed Barton Creek and the Colorado River (now Lady Bird Lake) is one of the city's largest recreational areas for water sports. Rob Greebon

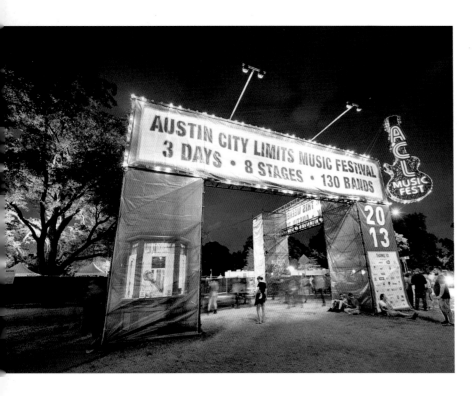

Above: In 1976, Austin PBS station KLRU began airing a weekly hour-long show spotlighting local and Texas performers who pioneered the city's music scene. Called *Austin City Limits,* it grew in popularity and drawing power, eventually gaining national recognition. The TV show led to the annual gathering "Austin City Limits Music Festival." The list of those who have appeared on the show and the music festival every October reads like a Who's Who of late twentieth-century and early twenty-first-century American musicians. John R Rogers

Right: Austin City Limits Music Festival, also known as ACL Live, has become one of the largest outdoor music events in the nation. Held in Zilker Park, this aerial shot shows a typical crowd for ACL Live—just one of almost 200 live music venues in the Austin-area, which is why this city is often referred to as the "Live Music Capital of the World." Rob Greebon

Above: Longhorn cattle by the thousands used to cross the undammed Colorado River just below Austin on the old Chisholm Trail. Some area ranches still maintain small herds of the breed that has become a Texas icon. John R Rogers

Left: Austin's exponential growth has covered much of Travis County, but traces of the area's more agrarian past—like this rusting cultivator—can still be found. John R Rogers

Above: With plenty of public land and not so much cash, Texas lawmakers bartered three million acres in the Texas Panhandle to the builders who oversaw construction of the Italian Renaissance Revival-style capitol. Work started in 1882 and continued for more than five years, using convicts and migrant workers to save money—although ordering custom doorknobs and hinges featuring the state's storied Lone Star apparently did not seem at all extravagant. Rob Greebon

Right: By the 1980s, the state's government had considerably outgrown the space available in the nineteenth-century capitol. Accordingly, lawmakers approved construction of a $75 million, four-story underground extension. Opened in 1993, the addition blends with the capitol's vintage architecture, mixing form with function. This image shows the statehouse before sunrise, viewed from the edge of the extension's open rotunda. Rob Greebon

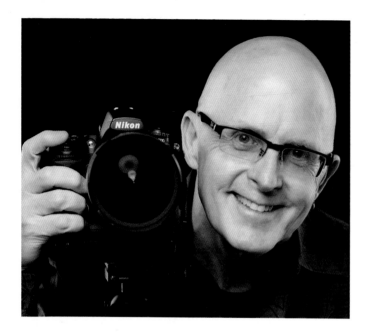

Since growing up in Austin and graduating from UT, **JOHN ROGERS** has been involved with professional photography and television production for over thirty years. After working for a national advertising agency producing and directing hundreds of corporate video productions, he opened his own business as a commercial photographer. His work has appeared internationally in magazines, textbooks, fine art galleries, and is displayed as large art pieces decorating spaces for companies including Google, Intuit, and Expedia.

"I love trying to capture and reveal the natural beauty of the person, place, or thing I am photographing. Very often I enhance my photographs to try and bring back to the viewer what they would experience if they were there."

You can see more of John's photographic art at www.JohnRRogers.com or contact him directly at John@JohnRRogers.com

ROB GREEBON is a 4th generation Texan who resides just outside of Austin in the Texas Hill Country with his wife and two daughters. As a self-taught photographer, Rob has successfully transitioned his love of the outdoors into an award-winning photography business. His work has been published internationally and appears regularly in local and national publications, television, and in many corporate and private collections.

As an admitted morning person, he enjoys the solitude and beauty that comes with a quiet sunrise, whether it's from a highrise in Austin or from a remote spot in the Texas Hill Country.

You can find more of Rob Greebon's photographs from Texas at www.ImagesfromTexas.com.

An elected member of the Texas Institute of Letters since 1993, **MIKE COX** is the author of twenty-seven non-fiction books. Over a freelance career of more than forty-five years, and a former award-winning reporter, he also has written hundreds of articles and essays for a wide variety of publications.

His best-selling work has been a two-volume history of the Texas Rangers published by Forge Books in New York. Another recent book, *Cowboy Stuntman: From Olympic Gold to the Silver Screen, the story of Dean Smith*, won three prestigious national awards, including a Will Rogers medallion in October 2014.

As a long-time Austin resident, Cox left the 8-to-5 world for good in February 2015 to write full time, and when not working, spends as much time as he can fishing and hunting.